Hotham Street Ladies
Ladies
A Book for Kids

HOTHAM STREET LADIES

A Book for KIDS!

ngv
National
Gallery of
Victoria

MELBOURNENOW

The National Gallery of Victoria sincerely thanks **the Dewhurst family** for their generous support, which has made the publication of this book for children possible.

This book belongs to

----

an artist in the baking!

About this book

The National Gallery of Victoria has worked with the Hotham Street Ladies to create this book about the artists' lives and the many cakes and works of art they have made. They share their stories about living in Melbourne and how the city inspires them. For you and your friends, there are lots of fun activities to do along the way.

Contents

Chapter 1

Meet the

HOTHAM STREET LADIES

We are a group of five artists.

We like to **make art that is interesting, funny** and **even a little bit disgusting.** We take the sorts of activities that old ladies do, like handicrafts and decorating cakes, and make them fresh and new.

Cassandra

Molly

Lyndal

Sarah

Caroline

Teamwork

We make our art **together**.

We build **sculptures out of cake** and we transform white art gallery spaces into rooms you'd usually see in a house. **We head outdoors to make street art** and publish **cookbooks** filled with stories and recipes collected from our friends and families.

Here are Caroline and Lyndal making street art in Germany.

Food for thought

Our art is about **life at home** and how food brings people together. It is also about our **friendship with one another** and what it's like to be a woman today.

Living in Melbourne **inspires us!**

Edible art

We don't use paints, brushes and canvas like many artists do. **We make art with food –** lots of cake, lollies, colourful icing and even gravy.

11

Chapter 2

HOME SWEET HOME

We gave this old room
a sweet makeover.

At different times over the years,
we've all lived in the same old house in Hotham
Street, in the Melbourne suburb of Collingwood.
That's why we call ourselves
the **Hotham Street Ladies!**

13

Crumbly house

The Hotham Street house is **very old**.
When we lived there years ago, the veranda was falling down, the concrete was cracked all around the outside and every room leant in a different direction.
If it rained outside, it rained inside too!

This is the house in Hotham Street.

It's important to all of us because it was once our home. Inside, every room was painted a different colour and the ceilings looked like they had been decorated with icing – a bit like a wedding cake.

What colour is your bedroom?

Show home

We made this cake especially for an art exhibition. It was displayed in the gallery on our kitchen table. We wanted the cake to look just like the real Hotham Street house – cracks and all.

Can you see a cat made out of icing? That's Henry!

Shoe biz

About one hundred years ago,
a shoemaker used to live in our house.
We found his old nails and tools in the back garden.

D.I.Y.

*Do it yourself

Make a picture of the front of your house using cake and icing.

Lollies, biscuits and wafers make great building materials! To get started, draw a picture of the front of your house and while you're drawing think about the lollies you need for the details.

Ask an adult for help.

YOU WILL NEED:

- A rectangular shaped cake – you could buy one pre-made, or bake at home – see page 78 for a cake recipe
- Icing – see page 77
- Food colouring
- Lollies, such as licorice allsorts and straps, mixed lollies and musk sticks, to create house features
- A piping bag
- A camera

INSTRUCTIONS:

1 While the cake is cooling, think about the colours of the walls and any extra details that you may want to add to your house cake.

2 Then, plan which lollies you will use to make the roof, doors and windows. For example, mini marshmallows could be bricks, slices of licorice allsorts could be window panes and musk sticks could be used for the doors. It's up to you! Look at pages 18–19 for more ideas.

3 Make a batch of icing and add food colouring to match the colours of your house.

4 When the cake is cool, transfer it to a plate. Then, take a flat knife and spread the icing over the top and sides.

5 While the icing is still sticky, decorate the top of the cake with different lollies.

6 Fill the piping bag with icing and use it to write your street name and house number next to the cake.

7 When you've finished, take a photo before everyone eats it!

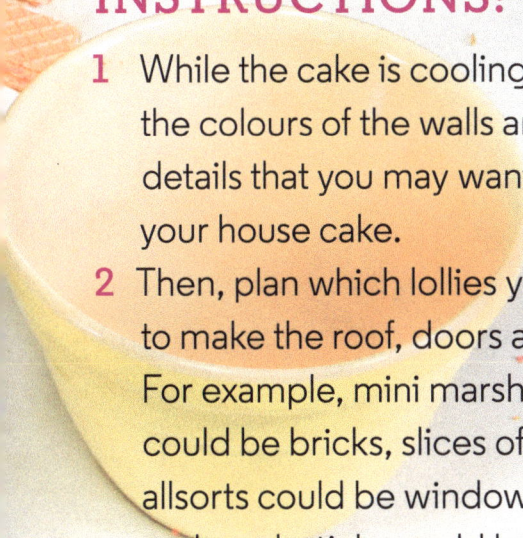

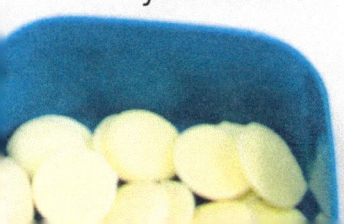

17

Chapter 3

SWEET

Did you know Melbourne is **famous for its street art?**

If you wander down some of the city laneways, you will see colourful spray-painted murals and art made with stencils all over the walls. It's like an outdoor art gallery!

A lot of **street art is about what's happening in the world today.** The artists paint imaginative pictures and write clever messages that make us laugh or think differently about things.

STREET

The Hotham Street Ladies at work in Collingwood, Melbourne.

Feeling peckish?

We made some big cardboard stencils of the letters H, S and L for Hotham Street Ladies. We placed the stencils on the footpath and filled the letter cut-outs with **lots of hundreds and thousands.** But the pigeons flew down and ate up all the hundreds and thousands before anyone had a chance to see our art.

They must have had sticky beaks!

GUESS WHAT?

Did you know that hundreds and thousands are made in a factory in Melbourne? **Inside every little ball is a tiny granule of sugar!**

Lyndal piping sausages and eggs on a barbecue.

Street food

When we make street art, we use cake icing instead of paints.

Why? Because it's fun and relates to ideas about home. Our street art doesn't last forever – we can create a big work of art and the next day rain washes it away …

D.I.Y.

*Do it yourself

Create your own street art with icing sugar and cake decorating tools.

Ask an adult to help you find a safe spot outside – a concrete path in a park is a good place to start. Other good spots are the backyard or the footpath in front of your house. Next, think of a message. You could try the initials of your name, your street or a combination of both to make a new word. During the holidays, why not tag 'MC' for Merry Christmas, or create a tag for Chinese New Year or Yom Kippur?

YOU WILL NEED:

- Paper stencil design – see page 76
- Icing sugar
- A sieve
- Icing mixture and piping bag – see page 77 for recipes and instructions
- Cake decorations, such as hundreds and thousands
- A camera

INSTRUCTIONS:

1 Head outdoors with all of the materials.
2 Place the paper stencil on the ground and tape it down.
3 With the sieve, dust the icing sugar lightly over the stencil to create a white shape.
4 Carefully remove the stencil to reveal the icing sugar shape. Don't worry if it's messy – the messy ones are the best.
5 With the piping bag, practise writing a couple of letters. Then, when you're ready, slowly pipe the letters onto the icing sugar.
6 Create a decorative border with any leftover icing and add some sprinkles.
7 Take a photo of your street art and send it to friends and family.

Chapter 4

LET'S PARTY!

Our table centrepiece of dirty dishes looks like the dinner party is over. But if you look at the place settings the knives and forks are clean. No one has eaten yet!

At Hotham Street **we loved having people over** for dinner and parties.

We liked making soups, pies and sausages, or whatever we felt like for dinner that night. Of course, there always had to be dessert.

You can **expect the unexpected** at one of our dinner parties.

Once, we were all having so much fun that **we woke up our neighbour.** He got out of bed and chased everyone around the backyard, waving a stick in the air. It was a funny sight because he was only **wearing his underpants!**

The Hotham Street Ladies dressed up to party!

A mistake with the steak

For another dinner party, we decided to make a tasty Moroccan dish. It was spicy meatballs with lots of tomatoes and minced beef. When we tasted the meatballs ... **they were disgusting.**

We had accidentally cooked the cat's pet food. **Poor Henry!**

Table talk

It's often the little accidents and silly things that make great stories to tell at dinnertime.

What funny things have happened at your place?

A crack-up

Another time, we made a surprise pudding for our dinner guests.

We mixed up the ingredients, popped the pudding in the oven and felt very pleased with ourselves. That is, until we spotted the eggs on the kitchen table! **We quickly pulled out the pudding and whisked in the eggs.** When the pudding was served, the guests loved it – even the lumps of egg!

GUESS WHAT?

In Melbourne you can catch a tram that is **also a fancy restaurant.** Its passengers travel along the streets, seeing the city sights, while enjoying dinner.

Feel the pinch

To celebrate the Melbourne Cup, we held an afternoon tea at Hotham Street. **We decorated the rooms with big vases of colourful roses.** At the time, we couldn't afford to buy flowers. So, in the middle of the night, we snuck out with scissors and **with a snippety-snip gathered flowers from our street.**

It was naughty, but we only took flowers from big bushes with plenty to share.

For a special event, we created a spectacular scene of a dinner party's leftovers. Can you see the chop bones? We made them with sugar paste, and the gravy was actually cake icing dyed brown.

33

D.I.Y.

*Do it yourself

Host a dinner party on the weekend! Try out some of these ideas and have fun at dinnertime with your family and friends.

THE MORE THE MERRIER

Invite some friends over for dinner. Perhaps they could bring along a dish that tells a story about their family. One of our housemates, named Bryan, came from a community near the Murray River in Victoria. When he returned from visiting his family, he'd often bring **kangaroo or even snake** for us to try.

DRESS UP

Be creative! Start by making a display on your table for everyone to admire. It could be an arrangement of your favourite things, or a vase of flowers picked from the garden.

PLACEMATS

Make placemats for your guests.
To get started, choose one of the border designs on pages 79–83 and make copies for everyone. Then draw pictures on them and include the menu. One of our friends serves cheese on biscuits and calls them 'mouse traps'. What creative names can you think of for different dishes?

Snowy

* Entreé :
  chicken with roast vegies
* Main :
  fried steak and gravy
* Dessert :
  dog food cake.

SET THE PET

If you have a pet, don't forget the most important member of the household.

Your little mate will feel special with a placemat made by you.

COUNTRY MUSIC

Select some songs to play during the dinner. If you're cooking Swedish meatballs you could play ABBA songs. What music would you play if you were having spaghetti bolognaise, fried rice or tacos?

FUNNY FACES

We love the messy scenes after a dinner party. When everyone has finished their meal, declare that it is time to **make faces with the leftover food** on their plates. Take photos of everyone's creations.

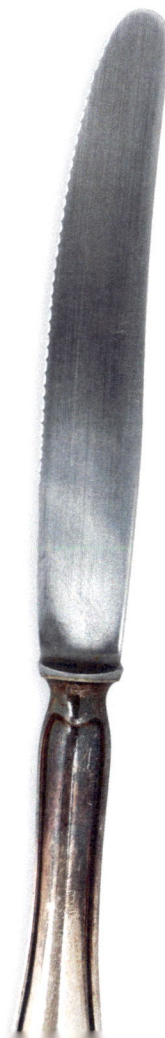

TOAST MASTER

A toast is a short speech made at the start of dinner. This speech helps make everyone feel happy being together.

Here's what to do. When you're about to speak, stand up and raise your glass. Then, make your speech and finish with a small cheer. Everyone will reply with a big cheer.

Here are some Hotham Street Ladies' toasts you might like to use:

'May our cakes **never fail!**'

'Live and let **eat!**'

'In pie, we **crust!**'

Chapter 5

GREEN SCENE

We made this big sculpture in the shape of a **wheelie bin** – the sort of bin that everyone has at their house. The sculpture is made of white wrought iron, which often appears on houses in the city. **Around the bin we planted flowers and vegetables.** We wanted them to grow and cover the sculpture so that it turned green.

People can see the bin on Hoddle Street as they travel through Clifton Hill. The sculpture reminds us to **look after the environment** by growing our own food, recycling and trying not to waste anything at home.

GREEN THUMBS DOWN

Every spring at Hotham Street we planted **herbs and veggies** in the backyard to use in our cooking. After all the excitement of planting the garden, we would get back to making art and forget all about it. The following year we would have to start all over again. **Looking after a garden is lots of work!**

Oops!

Have you noticed that sometimes things don't turn out how you imagined or planned they would? This can happen when you are **cooking, gardening or making art.** The fun part is thinking up new ideas or trying again.

After the gold rush in the 1850s, there was a big building boom in Melbourne. Many Victorian homes and buildings were **decorated with wrought iron at this time.** When you're next in the city, look around and spot the different wrought-iron patterns and decorations.

Homes and gardens

On quiet weekends at Hotham Street, we used to **stroll around the nearby streets to see what was growing in our neighbours' gardens**. We were inspired by all the different ways of growing plants and flowers. There were **gardens with flowers in neat rows,** while others were **higgledy-piggledy or overgrown.**

What do your neighbours grow in their gardens?

D.I.Y.

*Do it yourself

Why not grow a kitchen garden?

We had success in the garden growing **geraniums, cacti and succulents**. These are tough plants that don't need much attention or water. They grow well in **recycled pots**, such as **old tins, cracked vases, chipped coffee mugs** or even **old boots**! It was funny to see our old kitchen items sprouting leaves in the backyard.

To get started, **find an old container or buy an old pot** from a second-hand store.

Ask an adult for help.

YOU WILL NEED:

- Gloves and a gardening spade
- Newspaper
- A pot or container (make some drainage holes in the bottom if you can)
- Soil
- Herb seedlings or a succulent stem

INSTRUCTIONS:

1 Lay some sheets of newspaper on the ground.
2 Fill your container with soil.
3 Poke a hole in the soil with your finger and plant the seedling or stem in it.
4 Water and place the pot in a sunny spot. If you've planted a succulent, water it a little once a month, or every now and then.
5 Copy pages 79–83 and draw or paint your plant as it grows.

GREEN TIP

Did you know that some **succulents and geraniums** can grow from a small cutting? All you do is break off a short stem, plant it in soil and up it goes!

Chapter 6

ICING ON THE CAKE

When we started baking cakes, we had a lot to learn about cake decorating!

For inspiration, we visited shops that specialised in cake decorating equipment and started to collect old cake books. It surprised us to see **how many ways you can decorate a cake,** and how decorating styles have changed over the years.

We broke with the tradition
of a white wedding cake
for Caroline's big day and
made this big cat.

Sweet or savoury?

We challenge ourselves to make cakes that don't look like ordinary cakes. Once, we created **a cake that looked like a pizza!**

We went to a lot of trouble to make the pizza cake look realistic. There were **chunks of pineapple, bits of mushroom, and lots of melted cheese.** To complete the scene, we made a couple of greasy pizza boxes and a TV remote control.

Showtime

We entered our pizza cake into the Royal Melbourne Show cake competition.

It looked unusual next to all of the pretty cakes. We didn't win, but **we were proud of our cake** and enjoyed the experience.

Puppy love

Sculptures and paintings inspire our cake making, too.

One of our favourite creations is this cake shaped into a dog and covered in tiny, sugary flowers. The idea came from a huge sculpture of a dog covered with real flowering plants by American artist Jeff Koons.

True love

Caroline's wedding was a special occasion for all of the Hotham Street Ladies. Traditional wedding cakes are white and flowery, but because Caroline loves leopard-skin print, we created a **cake in the shape of a leopard.** For a **touch of bling** we gave the big cat false eyelashes **and fake diamonds in its teeth!**

D.I.Y.

* Do it yourself

Make paper flags and display them on top of a cake.

This is a great drawing activity for birthday parties. You could make a paper flag for each guest or set up the activity for everyone to do during the party.

YOU WILL NEED:

- Light-coloured cardboard or paper
- Coloured markers or pencils
- Scissors
- Bamboo skewers
- Glue
- A cake – see page 78 for a recipe to make one at home, or buy one from the shops
- A camera

INSTRUCTIONS:

1. Fold the piece of paper in half.
2. Draw a picture on one side of it, close to the folded edge.
3. With the scissors, cut around the drawing to make a shape, taking care not to cut across the fold.
4. Draw another picture on the back of the shape or write a short message – use lots of colours to make it spectacular!
5. At the fold, wrap the paper shape around a bamboo skewer and stick the two sheets together with glue. It should look like a small flag.
6. Make more flags and place them on top of the cake.
7. Before everyone takes a slice, take a photo!

Chapter 7

RECIPE FOR DISASTER

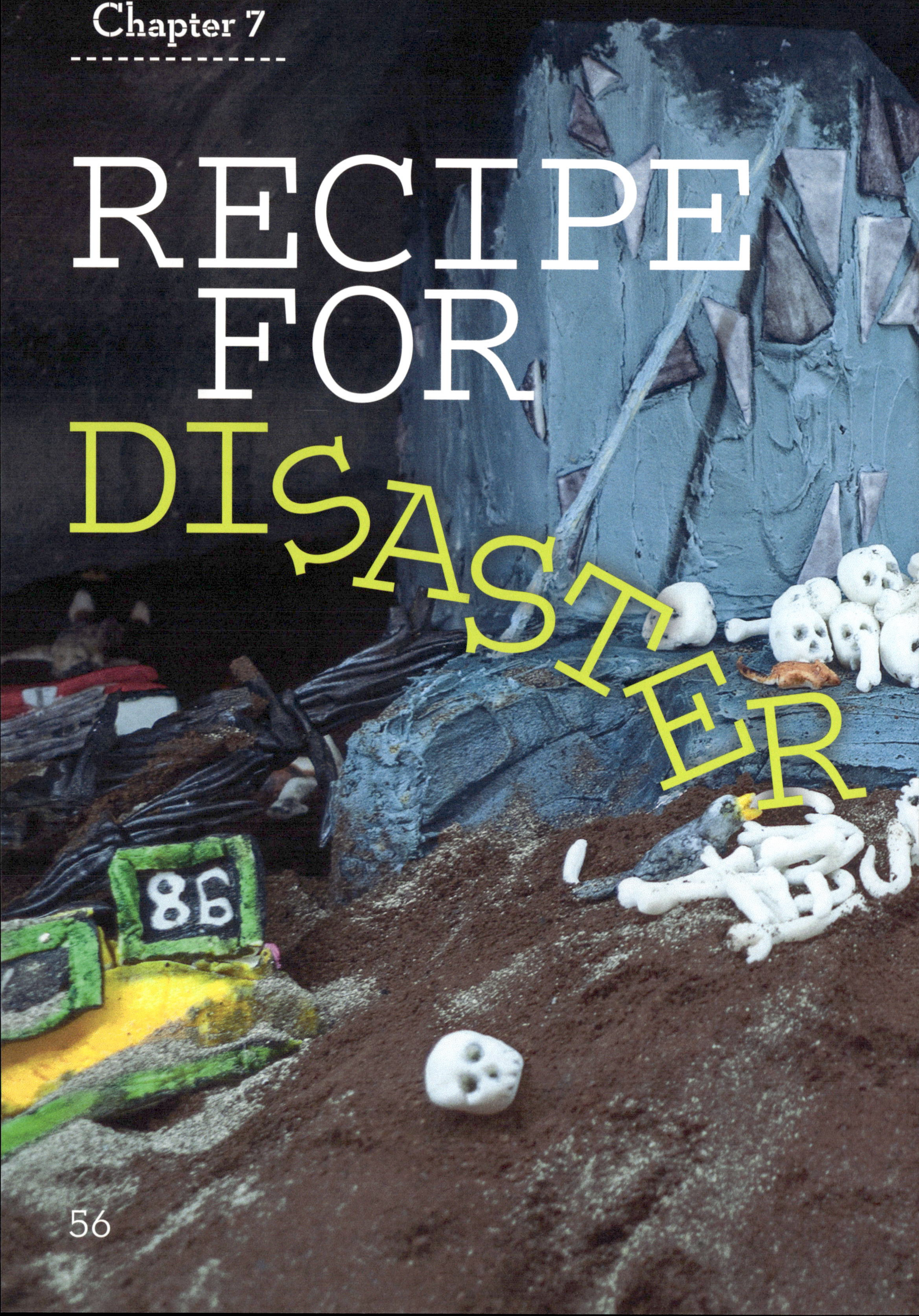

Doom and gloom! We made this spooky scene inside an old pizza oven. It was a bit creepy, with skulls, skeletons and rats made of icing.

That's revolting

Many cakes are **pretty and perfect**, but not the cakes made by the Hotham Street Ladies! We are inspired by things that are not very nice, such as **mould, mice, maggots** and **even vomit.**

We dressed as scientists when serving the Age-Defying Treasure Slice with Hidden Nutrient Particles.

Trash **or** treasure?

For a friend, we made a big cake in the shape of a mountain.

We filled it with treats and called it the **Age-Defying Treasure Slice with Hidden Nutrient Particles.**

We thought the cake was too ugly to eat, but we were wrong! When the first slice was cut, revealing treasure inside, people wanted more. Everyone enjoyed finding **Easter egg,** chunks of **blue coconut slice** and **chocolate crackle** inside the cake. It didn't take long for the mountain to disappear!

Pretty disgusting

The old wedding cake mentioned in the book *Great Expectations* by Charles Dickens inspired us to make one of our own. **After we had baked and decorated the cake, we set to work to make it look old and mouldy.** We broke off pieces, crumbled the edges and made lots of creepy crawlies. **When it was finished, it looked pretty – pretty disgusting that is!**

D.I.Y.

*Do it yourself

Create your own scene of doom and gloom with cake, icing and lollies. Make it as scary you can!

YOU WILL NEED:

- Baking tray
- Aluminium foil
- Chocolate cake for the soil – see page 78, or buy one from the shops
- Red jelly for the river of blood (make according to packet instructions)
- White icing fondant
- Food colouring
- Licorice straps and lollies

INSTRUCTIONS:

1 Line the tray with a piece of foil or baking paper.
2 For the river, make a rectangular container from foil to hold the red jelly.
3 Place the container onto the big tray and crumble chocolate cake all around it to make the soil. Remove any cake from the container that has fallen into it.
4 To create the river, chop up the red jelly and tip it into the container. Now your scene is ready …

61

It's time to add scary objects made from lollies and white fondant. Try some of these ideas ...

SKULLS

To make a skull, take a piece of fondant the size of a ping-pong ball and, using the end of a pencil or paintbrush, poke to create eye sockets. Next, make a triangular dent for the nose and a rectangular dent for the mouth. Use little pieces of licorice to fill the eye sockets and to add rotten teeth.

EYES

The little silver balls made from sugar you usually see on wedding cakes make great glinting eyes for a skull or slug!

TEETH

Make lolly teeth really ugly by removing a tooth, or by blackening them with food colouring.

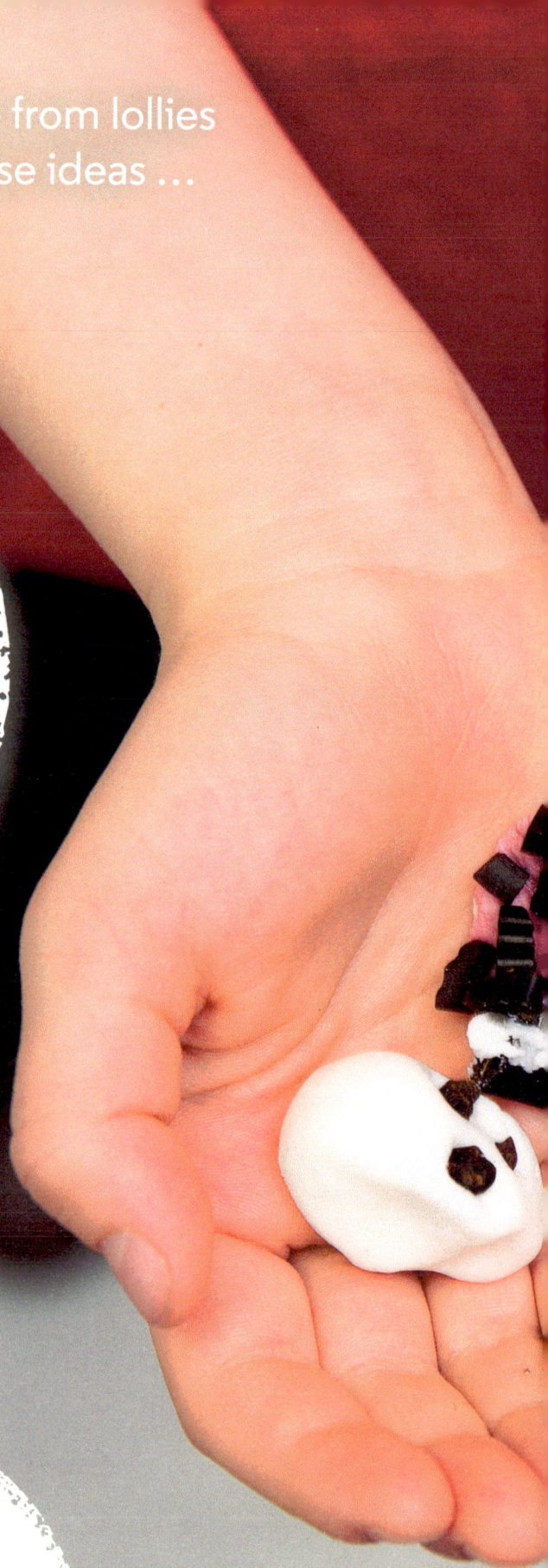

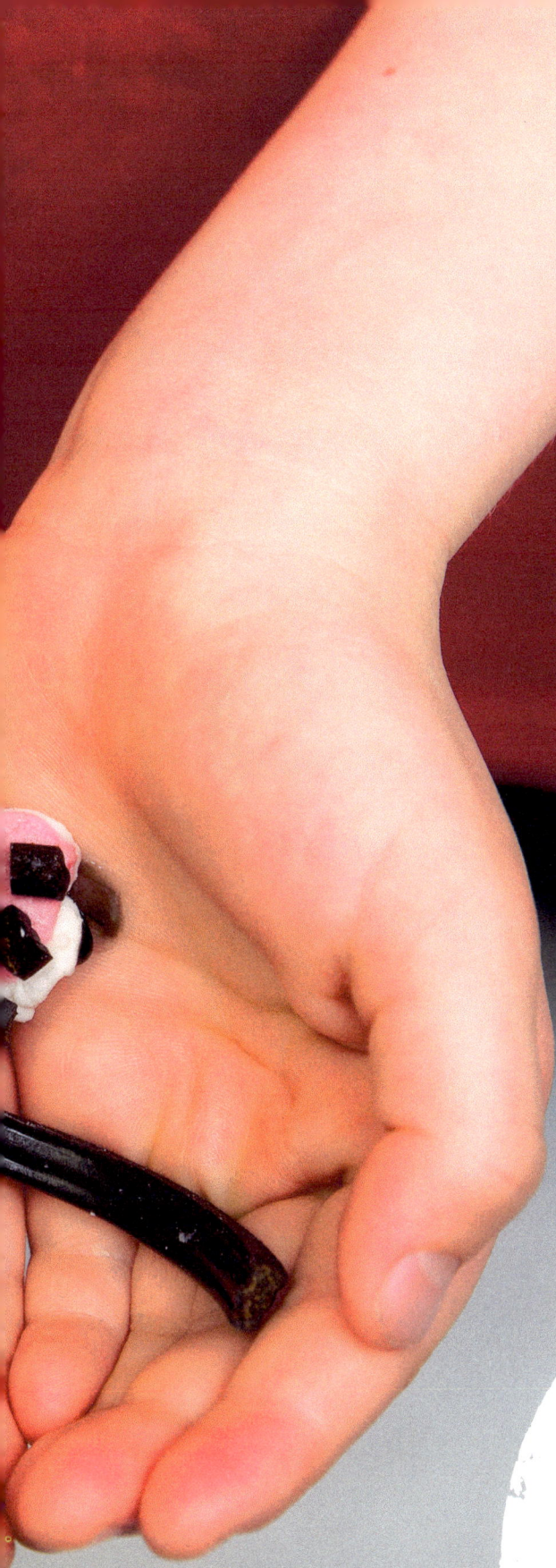

SLIME

Stretch and shape green lollies to make a disgusting pile of goop! Then make a fly or bug out of a piece of licorice to rest on top of the pile.

BONES, WORMS AND SLUGS

Roll the fondant into little sausage shapes to make bones, slugs and worms. Use small pieces of licorice or lollies to create eyes and tongues.

Chapter 8

RECIPES

Cook the books!

All the different dishes

that our families and friends have enjoyed together over many years inspired us to publish the **Hotham Street Ladies' recipe books.** We made lots of copies and gave them away at Christmas time.

FOR SUCCESS

Delicious dishes

Here are **some of our favourite recipes** for you to make.
Ask an adult to help you cook them.

H.S.L
Hotham Street Ladies'
Contribution Cookery Book

H.S.L
Hotham Street Ladies'
Tastes from the Shared
Kitchen

Cassandra's strawberry and watermelon salad

This fruit salad combines my love of **hot pink,** shopping at **Lebanese and Turkish grocery stores** and **'borrowing' roses** from my neighbours' gardens. The crystallised **rose petals** are easy to make if you have time.

Salad ingredients
- 1 punnet of strawberries, green tops removed, cut in half
- ½ watermelon, cut into chunks
- Handful of mint leaves, washed and finely chopped
- ½ teaspoon of rose water
- Turkish or Iranian fairy floss – vanilla and pistachio flavours are delicious
- Crystallised rose petals (optional)

Salad equipment
- Knife
- Chopping board
- Measuring spoons
- Colourful bowl

Crystallised rose petals ingredients (optional)
- 10 red or pink rose petals – roses that smell nice taste the best
- 1 eggwhite in a bowl
- ½ cup of caster sugar in a bowl

Crystallised rose petals equipment
- Clean tea towel
- Cake rack

Method
1 Combine the watermelon and strawberries in a bowl.
2 Add the mint and mix through the fruit.
3 To make the crystallised rose petals (optional), wash the rose petals carefully and place them on a clean tea towel.
4 Place the two bowls with sugar and eggwhite side by side.
5 Dip the petals in the eggwhite, and then in the sugar.
6 Place the petals on a cake rack to dry.
7 Lightly sprinkle rose water over the fruit – don't use too much.
8 Decorate the fruit with the petals and sprinkle lots of fairy floss on top.

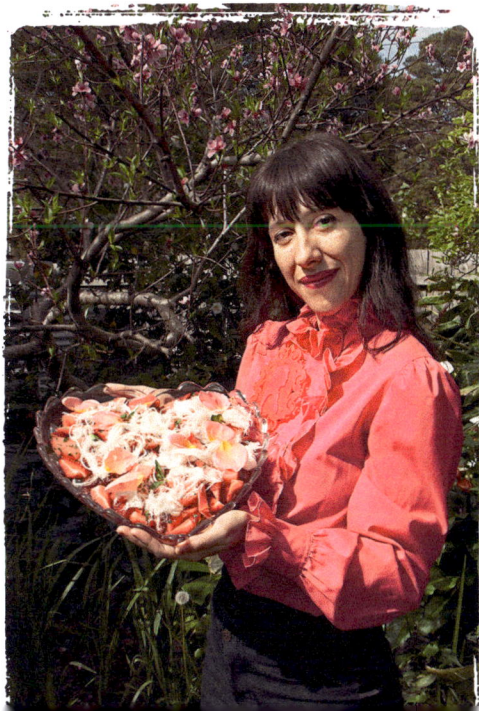

Caroline's frozen treats

Creamy mango pops are perfect to serve your friends on a hot day. They're good for you and taste like summer.

Ingredients
- 1 ½ cups of chopped mango
- 1 cup of Greek yoghurt
- 1 tablespoon of honey
- Pinch of salt

Equipment
- Food processor or blender (ask an adult to operate)
- Spoon and measuring cups
- Icy-pole moulds

Method
1 Mix all the ingredients together in a food processor or blender.
2 Pour mixture into icy-pole moulds and freeze overnight.

The next day, enjoy your creamy mango pops with friends!

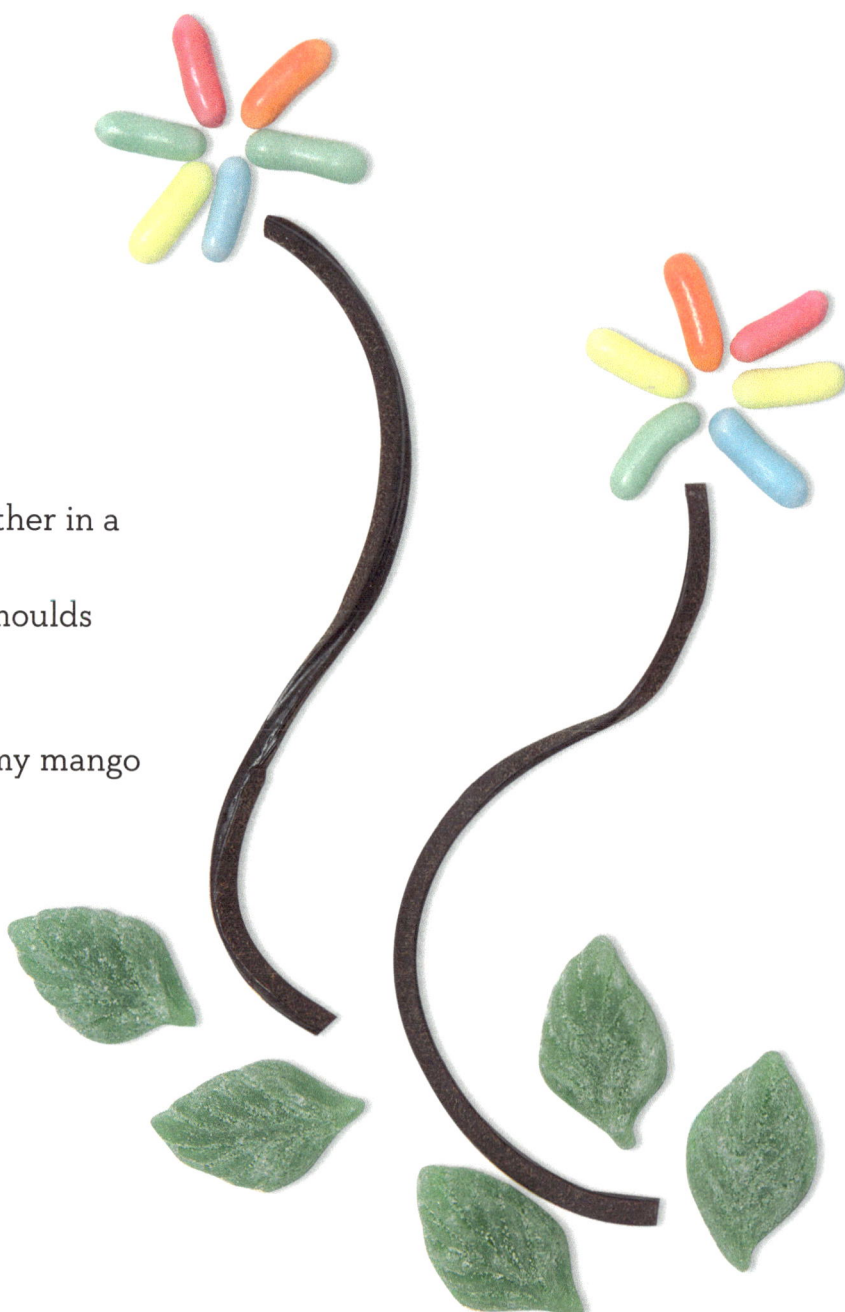

Sarah's rice paper rolls

These are **perfect for dinner on a hot summer night.** Prepare all of the ingredients, pop them on the table and let everyone take turns making their own rolls.

Ingredients

- 1 cucumber
- 1 carrot
- 2 finely chopped spring onions
- 1 red capsicum
- Handful of snow peas
- Bean sprouts
- Coriander leaves and/or Vietnamese mint leaves
- Cooked vermicelli noodles (follow packet instructions to prepare)
- Slices of barbecue chicken or pork (steamed prawns or fried tofu are delicious alternatives)
- Hoisin sauce
- Soy sauce
- Pack of 22 cm rice paper rounds (available from most supermarkets)

Method

1 Cut the vegetables into long, thin matchsticks.
2 Arrange the noodles, salad ingredients and cooked meat on plates and place in the centre of the dining table.
3 Take two small bowls to the table and pour a little Hoisin sauce in one, and some soy sauce in the other.
4 Ask an adult to fill a large bowl with hot water and carry it to the table.

Now you're ready to eat.

Instructions

1 Dip your rice paper into the hot water, then place on your plate. The paper will be hard at first but will soften after a short while.
2 Choose a few ingredients and place them in the centre of the rice paper.
3 Fold the paper as if you are wrapping a package.
4 Dip your rolls in the sauce and enjoy!

Lyndal's New Caledonian toast

Although this French toast recipe isn't really from New Caledonia, I call it 'New Caledonian toast' because people in that country **speak French and eat lots of mangoes** and other tropical fruits.

Ingredients

- 1 egg
- ¼ cup of milk (I like soy milk)
- 2 slices of bread
- 1 tablespoon of butter
- 1 mango

Equipment

- Knife and fork
- Bowl
- Frying pan
- Egg flip
- Measuring cup
- Plates

Method

1 Beat the egg and milk with a fork until they are well combined.
2 Put a piece of bread in the egg and milk mixture and press with a fork so the mixture soaks into the bread.
3 Heat the pan on medium heat, and melt the butter in it.
4 Place the slices of bread in the pan and fry each side until golden and the egg mixture is cooked.
5 Cut the mango into bite-size slices.
6 To serve, place the fried toast on a pretty plate, with the mango on the side.

Molly's jelly snakes in a lake

Create a lake scene with blue jelly for water and creatures made out of lollies. To get started, buy some lollies that you would like to see in the jelly water. **Chocolate frogs** and **jelly snakes** work well; so do fruit strips or Roll-Ups when cut into shapes of **fish**, **seaweed** and **lily pads**.

Ingredients
- Fruit strips
- 2 packets of blue jelly crystals
- A selection of lollies

Equipment
- Clear glass or clear plastic bowl
- Measuring jugs
- Butter knife
- Chopping board

Method
1 Cut the fruit strips into seaweed, fish and lily pad shapes.
2 Make the blue jelly following the instructions on the packet.
3 Pour it into the clear bowl and leave until it is cool, but not set.
4 Drop the fish, frogs, snakes and some of the seaweed into the cooled jelly.
5 Place the bowl in the fridge and leave for a couple of hours, or until the jelly has set.
6 Finally, pop the lily pads on top of the jelly lake and place it on the table for everyone to see!

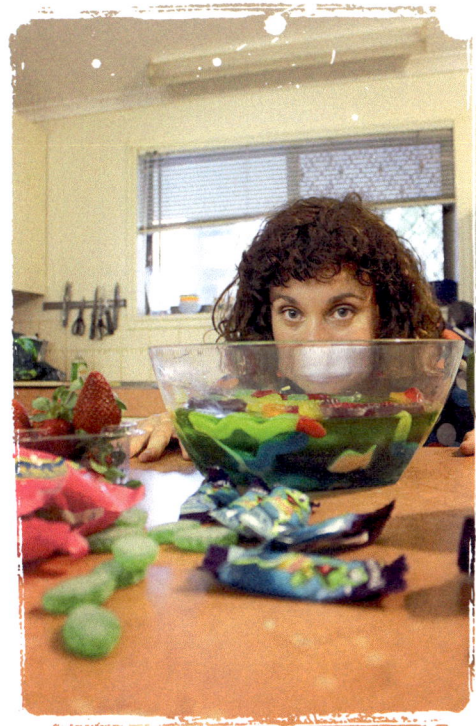

D.I.Y.

essentials

*Do it yourself

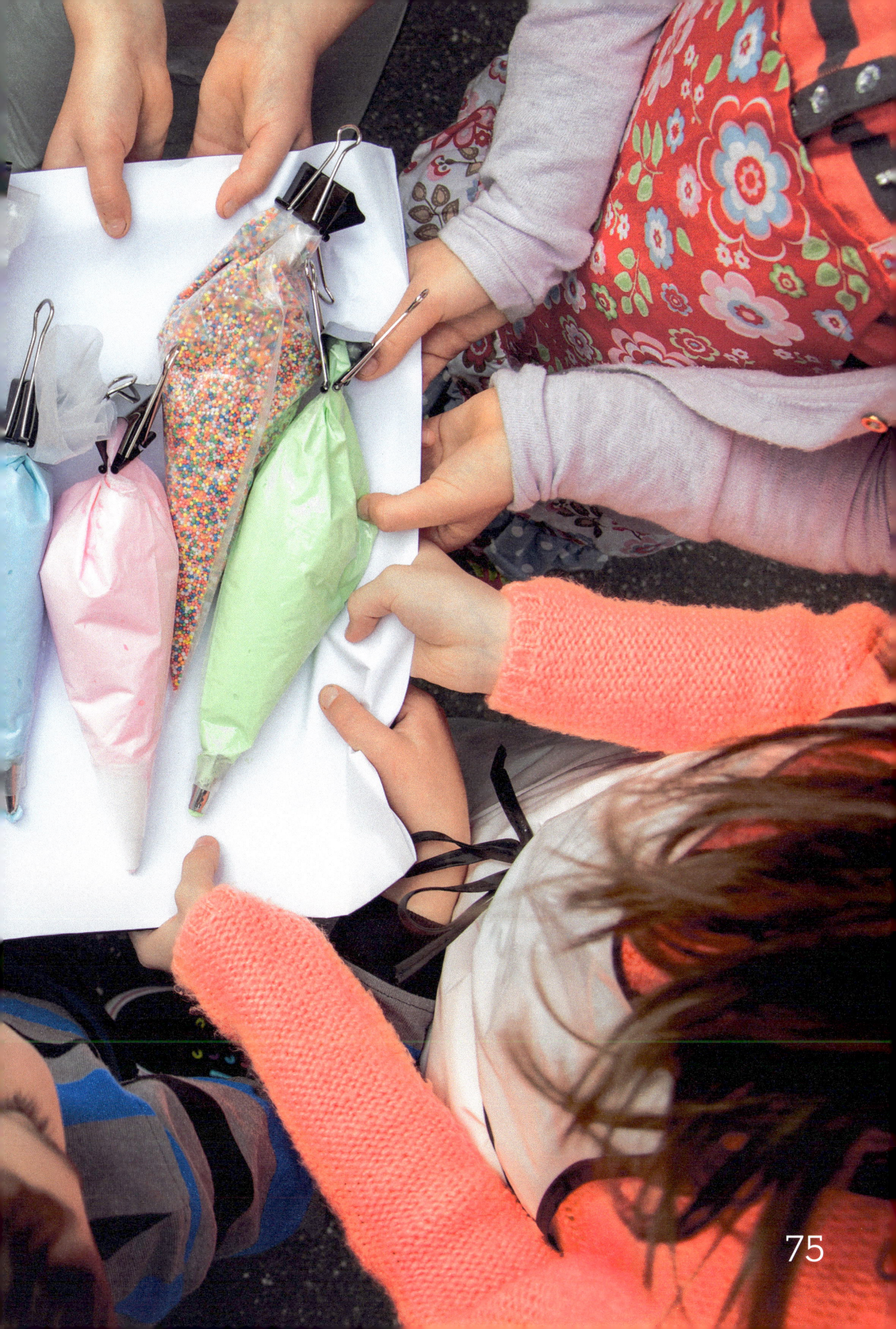

Street art stencil

Some street artists like to use stencils, which allow them to repeat their designs quickly and simply. Here is an easy way to make your own paper cut-out stencil. Use it to create a background for your sugary tag.

You will need:
- A4 sheet of paper
- Pencils
- Scissors
- Tape

Instructions

1 Fold the A4 sheet of paper in half lengthways.
2 Think of a simple shape, such as a circle, square or heart and, starting at the fold, draw half of it on the paper.
3 Cut out the shape with scissors then open up the sheet of paper. This is your stencil for making street art!
4 Now go to page 24 for instructions for what to do next.

Royal icing

You can buy ready-made packets of royal icing, or you can make your own.
Ask an adult for help.

Ingredients
- 1 eggwhite
- 2 cups of icing sugar
- $\frac{1}{2}$ teaspoon of lemon juice
- Food colouring

Equipment
- Electric mixer
- Bowls
- Spatula or wooden spoon
- Piping bag and nozzle tips – available from most supermarkets

Method
1. Beat the eggwhite in the mixer while gradually adding the icing sugar.
2. Continue to beat the icing until it has thickened and can hold its shape.
3. Add the lemon juice and beat well again. Cover with plastic wrap and set aside until your cake is ready to decorate.
4. If you wish to make piping of different colours, divide the icing mixture into separate bowls.
5. Add drops of food colouring and mix well.
6. With a spoon, scoop the first mixture into the bag and push it to the bottom. Hold the bag with both hands, as if it was a big pencil, and squeeze its top gently until icing comes out of the nozzle tip.

Practise piping on a plate before starting your work of art! Clean out the bag and repeat step 6 to apply different colours.

77

Chocolate cake recipe

This chocolate cake is easy to make and works perfectly every time!
Ask a grown-up for help.

Ingredients
- 1 cup of water
- 2 cups of sifted plain flour
- 2 cups of caster sugar
- 2 eggs
- $\frac{1}{2}$ teaspoon of baking powder
- 1 $\frac{1}{4}$ teaspoons of baking soda
- 4 tablespoons of cocoa
- $\frac{3}{4}$ cup of sour cream
- 80 g of unsalted butter at room temperature
- $\frac{1}{2}$ teaspoon of salt

Equipment
- 24 cm cake tin (springform tin works well)
- Baking paper
- Measuring cups and spoons
- Scales
- Electric mixer
- Cake rack

Method
1 Preheat oven to 160 °C.
2 Grease the base of the cake tin and line it with baking paper.
3 Put all the ingredients in an electric mixer and mix on slow speed for 2 minutes.
4 Stop the mixer, scrape the sides and then mix at full speed for 2 minutes.
5 Pour the cake mixture into the cake tin and bake for 50–60 minutes.
6 Let the cake sit for 10 minutes, then turn it onto a cake rack to cool.

Use this for creating a doom and gloom scene (pages 60–3), or as the base for a house cake (pages 16–17).

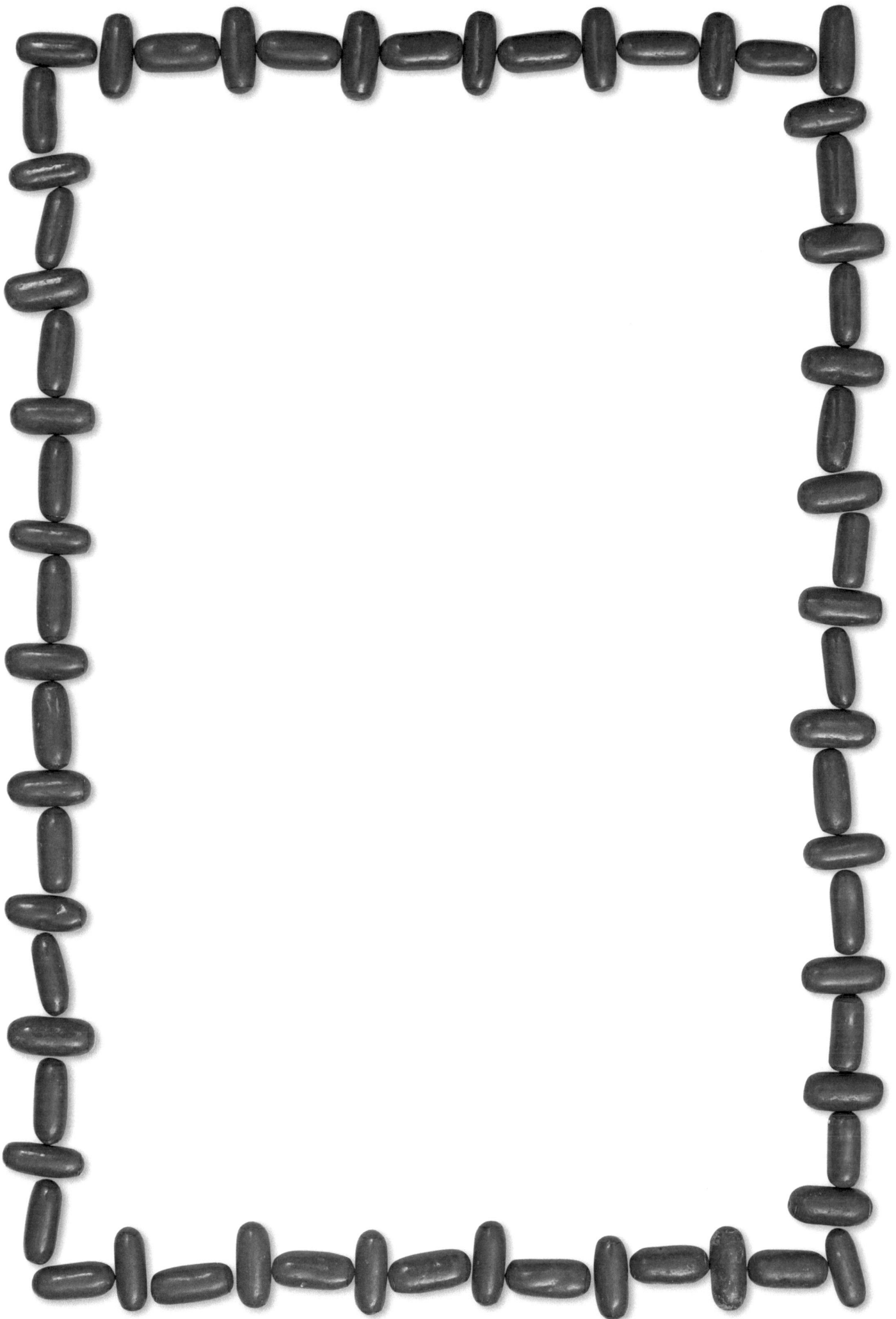

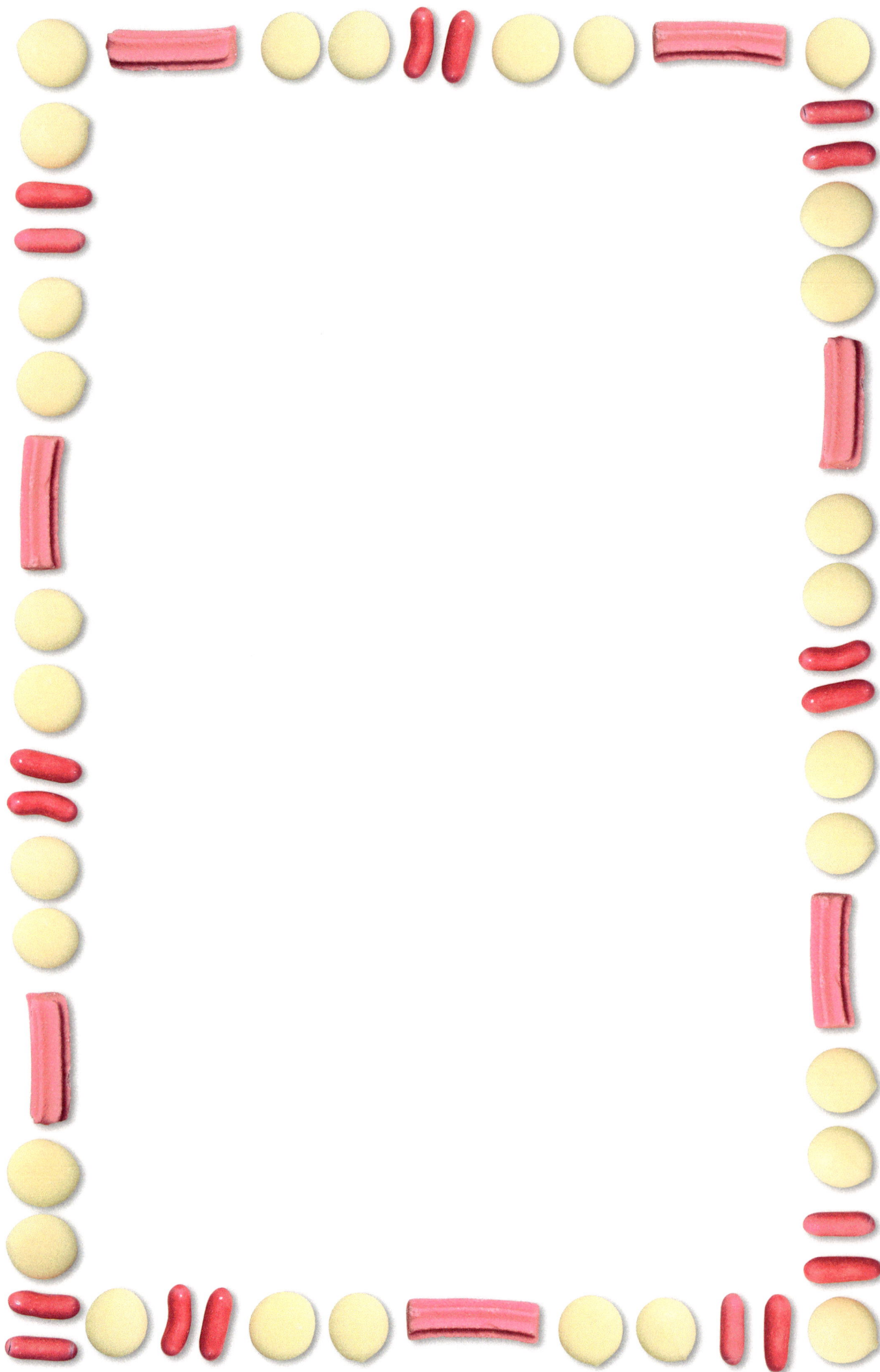

List of works

Hotham Strasse Damen Berlin, 2011

Caroline and Lyndal were both in Berlin so they made some street art to celebrate and show the ladies at home.

--------→

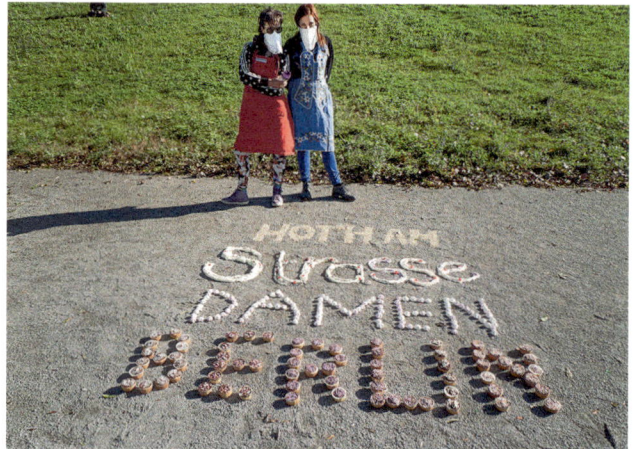

Sweetening the Dosshouse, 2009

We decorated this hotel room at The Carlton Hotel when it was still very rundown for an exhibition called *Girls Girls Girls*, which included thirty-five female artists.

←--------

Hotham Street House cake, 2008

We made this cake, our first art project, for an exhibition called *Group Group Show* curated by Damp at the Victorian College of the Arts Margaret Lawrence Gallery. All the work in the show was made by groups of artists who make their work together.

--------→

Tote spew, 2013

This work was photographed and shown in *Backflip*, an exhibition about feminism and humour held at the Victorian College of the Arts Margaret Lawrence Gallery.

Sausage sizzle for Leinster Arms, 2013

This work was photographed and shown in *Backflip*, an exhibition about feminism and humour held at the Victorian College of the Arts Margaret Lawrence Gallery.

Luxury with leftovers, 2013

The National Gallery of Victoria asked us to make a table setting for a dinner to raise funds for the NGV's Women's Association. We made everything out of icing and while the guests ate their dinner they sat around this scene of leftovers.

Hotham Street Ladies host dinner, 2011

As part of the Melbourne Food and Wine Festival, we hosted a share household dinner at the Panama Dining Room.

Green bin, 2011

We were commissioned by the City of Yarra to make a work about food sustainability. This work is on Hoddle Street in Clifton Hill.

- - - - - - →

Pizza cake, 2009

We made this cake to submit to the Royal Melbourne Show cake decorating competition.

← - - - - - - -

Puppy cake, 2011

We were asked by the artist-run gallery West Space to make a cake to celebrate the opening of their new gallery in Bourke Street. The cake was inspired by *Puppy*, 1992, by Jeff Koons.

- - - - - - →

Leopard wedding cake, 2010

We made this enormous wedding cake for Caroline and her husband Hugh.

- - - - - →

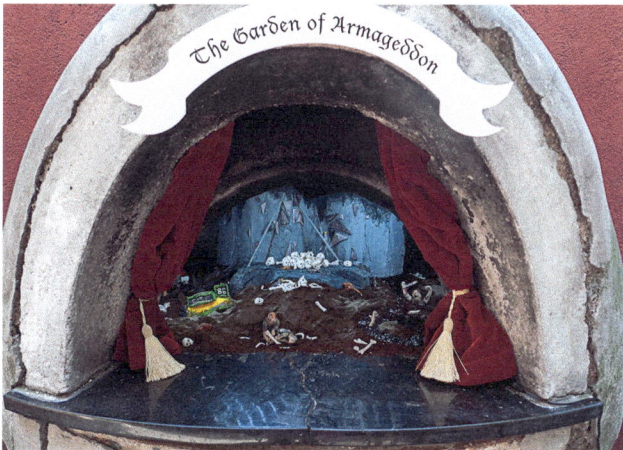

The Garden of Armageddon, 2010

We were commissioned by West Space to make this work at Sarti Restaurant and Bar.

← - - - - -

Age-Defying Treasure Slice with Hidden Nutrient Particles, 2012

We made this work to accompany our friend jeweller Nicholas Bastin's exhibition at Craft. It was inspired by one of his works.

- - - - - →

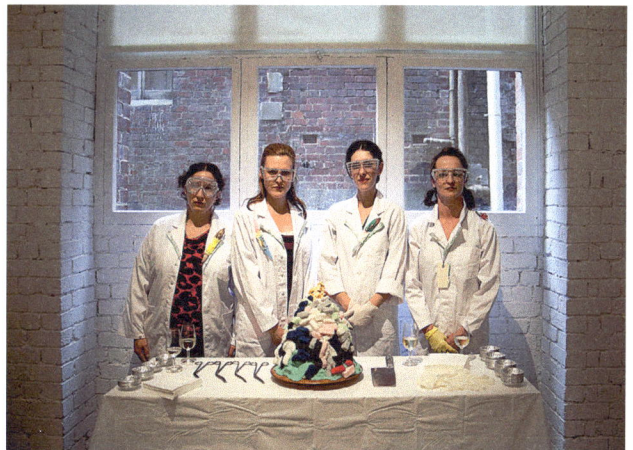

Miss Havisham cake, 2010

We made this work for the Royal Melbourne Show cake decorating competition. It was inspired by Miss Havisham's wedding cake in Charles Dickens' novel *Great Expectations*. It was disqualified for being in poor taste.

← - - - - -

Thanks

Executive management team
Tony Ellwood, Director
Andrew Clark, Deputy Director
Isobel Crombie, Assistant Director, Curatorial
    and Collection Management

Publication team
Tony Ellwood, Director
Andrew Clark, Deputy Director
Don Heron, Head of Exhibitions Management,
    Design and Multimedia
Kate Ryan, author
Jasmin Chua, Publications Manager
Jennie Moloney, Senior Publications Coordinator
Thomas Deverall, Senior Designer
Mark Gomes, Editor
Christian Markel and Selina Ou, Photographers
Justine Frost and Anne-Marie De Boni, Prepress -
    Imaging Technicians
Katie Somerville, Curator, Australian Fashion and Textiles
Yvette Pratt, Family and Community Program Coordinator

Additional photography: Predrag Cancar pp. 20-1, pp. 28-9,
p. 33; Thomas Deverall p. 14, pp. 40-1, p. 43; iStock Photos
p. 37, p. 42.

Cover stock: 150gsm Hanno Gloss
Endpapers: 150gsm Precision
Text stock: 150gsm Precision
Printer: Southern Colour (VIC)

The National Gallery of Victoria would like to thank
the Hotham Street Ladies: Cassandra Chilton, Molly
O'Shaughnessy, Sarah Parkes, Caroline Price and Lyndal
Walker, for their creativity, photographs and delightful
works of art, which feature throughout this publication.

We are also grateful to the following children who participated
in the photo shoots for the book: Spike Angwin, Milly Clark,
Nina Gillespie, Oscar Gillespie, Judie Goldman, Laura Heron,
Georgia Kent, Oliver Moore, Charlotte Pratt, Lachlan Pratt
and Archie Somerville.

The Hotham Street Ladies would like to thank Victoria
Bennett, Concettina Inserra, Scott McCormack, Matthew
Read and Hugh Thorn.

*The National Gallery of Victoria sincerely thanks Melbourne
Now Champions the Dewhurst family for their generous
support, which has made the publication of this book for
children possible.*

*The NGV's children's programs are supported by the Truby
and Florence Williams Charitable Trust.*

First published in 2013 by
The Council of Trustees of
the National Gallery of Victoria
180 St Kilda Road
Melbourne, Victoria 3004, Australia
www.ngv.vic.gov.au

Published for the exhibition *Melbourne Now*,
NGV International, 180 St Kilda Road, Melbourne,
and The Ian Potter Centre, NGV Australia,
22 November 2013 - 23 March 2014.

National Library of Australia Cataloguing-in-
Publication entry:

Author: Ryan, Kate, author.
Title: Hotham street ladies : a book for kids / Kate Ryan.
ISBN: 9780724103799 (hardback)
Target Audience: For primary school age.
Subjects: Interactive art—Victoria—
    Melbourne—Juvenile literature.
    Food in art—Exhibitions.
    Melbourne (Vic.)—Exhibitions.
Other Authors/Contributors:
    Chilton, Cassandra, 1974-
    O'Shaughnessy, Molly, 1973-
    Parkes, Sarah, 1977-
    Price, Caroline, 1970-
    Walker, Lyndal, 1973-
    National Gallery of Victoria.
Dewey Number: 708.99451

State Government
Victoria